You and Your

EMOTIONS

What Causes Them?

Understand Them for Better Health, Performance and Relations

James J. Barrell and Art Maynor

Acknowledgements

Special thanks to the people that made major contributions to this work.

Donald D. Price PhD – Emotion Research Expertise

James E. Barrell PhD – Conceptual Contributions

Donald C. Medeiros PhD – Experiential Method

Suzanne K. Sindledecker MA, MBA – Reviewer

FOREWORD

Do our emotions follow simple principles that we can understand by looking at our experiences? This brilliant little book asks the reader to look at how people experience the most common emotions of everyday life. It turns out that our desires and expectations fuel our emotions but we usually don't notice their influence because we are too immersed in the feelings themselves.

In this book, we can step back and look at the emotions of comic book characters. By noticing how the characters experience emotions across a wide variety of situations, we can begin to see how our own emotions are created. There is more than a century of attempts to clarify emotions through theories generated from considerable scientific effort. This book takes us beyond theories to a practical understanding of common emotions in everyday experiences which can be verified by science.

Dr. Donald Price
Neuroscience and Psychology
University of Florida

EMOTIONS

This book is about emotions.

Your mind is a "machine" that can create good or bad feelings.

You will learn about the "mechanics" of emotions.

You will understand how your "mind/machine" works and make your own choices.

You can choose to feel good or bad.

It is all up to you. You are responsible for your feelings and are no longer a victim.

The consequences of ignoring our emotions are enormous. Serious mental and physical illnesses can be based on emotional issues. We pay an outrageous price in health care due to a lack of understanding the human emotions. After all, the emotions are the bridge between the mind and body. Moreover, emotional understanding can also help build more positive relationships and enhance performances at any level.

* All pages are organized for left and right brain dominant readers. When there are cartoons, the left page is script and the right page is cartoons. It might be best to go from cartoon to script and then back and forth between script and cartoons for understanding.

2

INTRODUCTION

This may be one of the most important books you will ever read. Your emotions can make you healthy and happy or unhealthy and unhappy. In fact they can actually kill you.

You will learn what causes these emotions. These causes are not outside you. They are inside you. Whatever the outside situation is, it cannot cause an emotion. It is your inside reaction that causes it. But you are not responsible for this reaction until you understand what causes it. Once you know the cause then you can choose to feel good or bad.

This book is all about *good emotions* and *bad emotions.* By using good and bad, we do not mean that the emotions are right or wrong and that you should or should not have them. We simply mean that these emotions *feel* good or *feel* bad to us. Here is a listing of the common emotions that we will cover.

Good Emotions	Bad Emotions
Joy	Anxiety
Satisfaction	Frustration
Relief	Anger
Excitement	Depression

This book is all about these 8 common emotions. You will find them in many different situations (driving a car, on the job, being alone, going to school, taking a test, being at the doctor's office and so on). It doesn't matter what the situation is, there are different emotions that can happen. *Remember, the situation does not cause the emotion.* The cause is inside you! It is your reaction. Let us find out how this happens.

THE CART, HORSE, DRIVER AND OBSERVER

Here is a way to visualize the relationships between your emotions, mind/brain and body. The cart is the body. The horse is the emotions. The driver is the mind/brain which includes *who you think you are.* The observer oversees it all. It is "stepping outside of yourself" and being aware of what is happening in the moment.

The driver just wants to feel good and not feel bad. Although the horse is always looking for directions, the driver often just lets it take over and run the show. At those times, your observer is fast asleep. What happens? The cart is run off the road, the wheels can start to come off and the cart becomes damaged.

Instead of turning over control to the horse (emotions), the driver (mind-brain) needs to *wake up* the observer to get the information on how to take charge of the horse (emotions) and prevent the destruction of the cart (body). Only when the driver takes instructions from the observer can you be truly rational and have real choices in your life.

In this book you will become the observer of your mind/brain and emotions. This will allow you to direct the horse and drive your cart.

KEY POINTS

You can learn to choose and control your emotions. You can do this by understanding their *root causes*. This is not simply coping with them or applying bandages. To prove these causes to yourself, you have to strengthen the observer. The observer is <u>not</u> your thinking mind. Rather, the observer is that part of you that can simply be *aware* and notice your thoughts and feelings without judging them. Slowing down and being quiet will help you in this process. The observer will allow you to see how DESIRES, EXPECTATIONS and EMOTIONS work together. (Pages 4-7)

THE MOVEMENT TOWARD EMOTION

The fellow sees something that is important to him. Next he wants it. He checks to see if he can buy it. He has the money and believes he can buy it. Finally, he buys it and feels good.

This shows you how emotions can be created. Your value is part of your want or *desire*. Then you have a belief about whether or not you can get it. This is your *expectation*. Then a feeling or *emotion* can emerge.

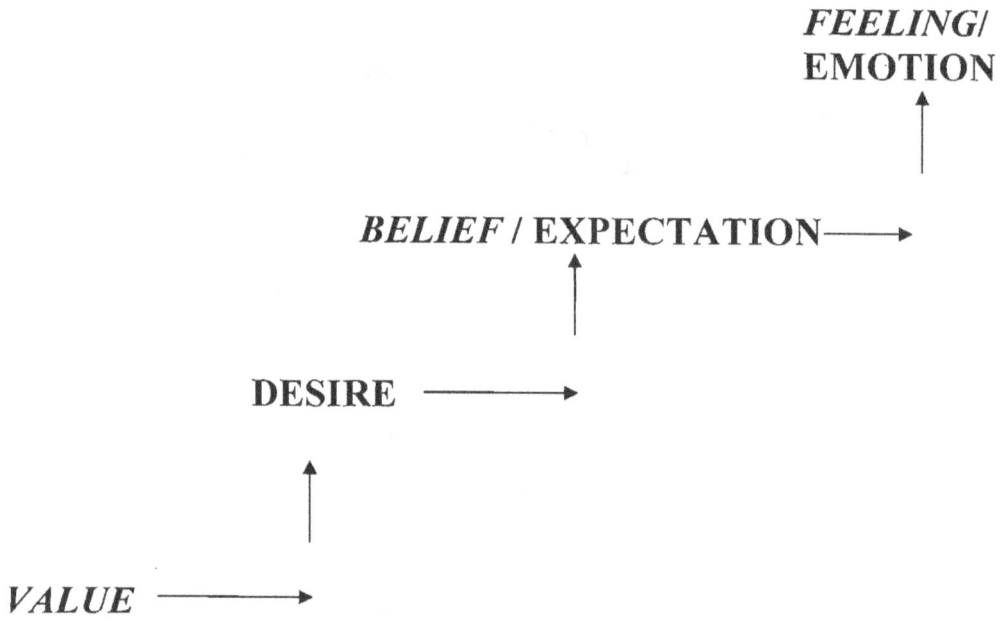

Value

Desire

Belief

Feeling

DESIRES AND EXPECTATIONS

What you want and what you expect are two different things. We can easily confuse them. But seeing them separately will help you discover how your emotions are created. Desires and expectations are at the root of emotions.

Is it desire or expectation?

Both of the fellows want the goal - a trophy in this case. This is a positive goal. It is something that both want. However, the fellow on the left is thinking about whether or not he can get it. He is expressing *expectation*. On the other hand, the fellow on the right is imagining how nice it would be to have it. He simply has a pure *desire*. Do you see the difference? *How much you want something (desire) is not the same as what you think your chances are of getting it (expectation).*

It is the combination of the desire and the expectation that creates the emotion. And remember a desire can relate to the future or past as well as the present. You may want something in the future or may *want to have had something in the past*. It doesn't matter. If you have an emotion, desire for you is *right now*.

What about when you have a <u>negative goal</u> instead of a positive goal? This is something that you want to <u>not</u> have happen or have happened. Look at the two ladies viewing the headlines of the paper. The lady on the left is considering whether or not she will get the flu. She is involved with *expectation.* Meanwhile the lady on the right is focused on not wanting to get the flu and getting a shot. She is preoccupied with her *desire.*

Of course, desires and expectations can occur in the same person and relate to any goal. We chose a trophy and a flu epidemic simply as examples.

Emotions are all about desire and expectation!

What are your expectations of getting a ticket?

Look at the line of all those people trying to get a ticket to a very *desirable* event. Each person in line has an *expectation* as to whether or not he or she will be getting a ticket. One person has a ticket in hand. He is very happy. Another further back feels confident she will get one and feels excited. In the middle of the line is a woman who is just not sure and is feeling anxious. Still back a little further is a fellow who is feeling frustrated. Toward the end of the line are a man who is angry and finally a man at the end of the line who has given up in depression.

All the people in line, feeling these emotions, have a desire. How much you want something *(desire)* is like turning the volume up on your emotions. It governs the intensity of your feelings.

Now look back at the people in line. Do you see how their *expectations* (of their chances of getting a ticket) determine the type of emotion that they will have and whether they will feel good or bad?

THE EMOTION MACHINE
Good Emotions and Bad Emotions

Your emotions are created by the mind/brain. The mind/brain is your emotion machine. What *expectation* will you dial up on your emotion machine? Will it result in a good feeling or a bad feeling? On one end of the dial you are certain you will get what you want and on the other end you feel certain that you will <u>not</u> get what you want. Joy, satisfaction and relief lie on one end while frustration, anger and depression lie on the other. In the middle you are just not sure one way or the other. Maybe you will or maybe you won't get what you want. At this point there is excitement or anxiety.

All these emotions happen when your *desire* to get what you want is strong. But what happens if you turn the desire intensity knob on your machine up or down? If you do this, each of your emotions will be felt slightly differently. For examples, depression can go up to despair or down to resignation, anger can go up to rage or down to disgust, anxiety can go up to terror or down to worry and joy can go up to bliss or down to simple happiness. How much you desire or want something controls how intensely you will feel the emotion.

Desire and Expectation – good feelings and bad feelings

It's your choice!

KEY POINTS

What about DESIRE? DESIRES can have <u>positive</u> or <u>negative goals</u>. That is, you can either <u>want</u> something to happen or you <u>want to avoid</u> something happening.   A goal is a part of your desire. You do not want without wanting something. When you have a goal you must also have a desire. (Pages 10-13)

DESIRE relates to the intensity of your emotion. When you turn up the intensity of your desire for something, you also turn up the intensity of your emotion. Interestingly, if you desire or want something too much and become preoccupied with it, your desire can turn into a negative goal. In other words, you may have wanted something at first but now you really need it. (Pages 12-15)

We all share a set of common emotions. It is your EXPECTATIONS related to a particular DESIRE that will largely determine which emotion you will feel in any given situation. Will it be a good or a bad feeling? Take the situation where you really want or need something. You have a strong desire. If you have very high expectations that you are getting, have gotten or will get what you want then you are likely to be feeling JOY, SATISFACTION or RELIEF. Instead your expectations may be very low. This is when you feel that you are not getting, have not gotten or will not get what you want. Now you will likely feel FRUSTRATION, ANGER or DEPRESSION. Finally, there are those times when you are just not sure you will get what you really want or need. You are filled with uncertainty. At this time the most likely emotions are EXCITEMENT or ANXIETY. (Pages 14-17)

18

ANXIETY AND EXCITEMENT CAN BE A CLOSE CALL

You can be shaking, nervous, tense and up tight. These are all signs of *anxiety*. This does not feel good. Many health problems can result from this emotion.

Then there are times when you feel all wired-up and tense but you feel good. You are excited! Sometimes this feels close to anxiety and it is. When you are both anxious and excited you are looking ahead. Maybe even imagining what could happen. There is uncertainty. Maybe this will happen or maybe it won't.

So what is the difference between anxiety and excitement? With anxiety you are focused on what you don't want to happen (a negative goal) and maybe even imaging the possible negative outcome. With excitement you are focused on what you do want to happen (a positive goal) and likely imaging a possible positive outcome. That is the only difference. It is your desired goal that makes the difference. It is not your expectation since in both cases you are uncertain.

Anxiety = negative goal + uncertain expectation

Excitement= positive goal + uncertain expectation.

It is what you want or DESIRE (a positive goal or a negative goal) that makes the difference in this close call.

Let us look at some familiar situations, that include *anxiety, excitement* and uncertainty.

EXCITEMENT AND ANXIETY

Don't be confused. Excitement and anxiety are not the same. Let us look at some familiar situations.

What about the driver and the passenger in the car?

The driver sees the risk and *uncertainty* in the driving but *wants* to take it as a challenge for himself. His *desire* is focused on the *positive*. The passenger also sees the risk and *uncertainty* in the drive but *wants* to avoid an accident. His *desire* is focused on the *negative*. The driver is *excited* and the passenger is *anxious*.

<u>Is the roller coaster fun or not?</u>

One person *wants* the thrill of feeling *uncertain* and being out of control. His *desire* is focused on the *positive.* The other person *wants* to avoid the *uncertainty* and all the terrible things that could happen. His *desire* is focused on the *negative.*

Is there pressure on the free throw line?

One player is thriving on the *uncertainty* of the situation. He is confident and *wanting* to make the winning shot. His *desire* is focused on the *positive.* The other player is shaking with the *uncertainty* and *wanting* to avoid missing the shot and losing the game. His *desire* is focused on the *negative.*

There you have it! Both anxiety and excitement can have *uncertainty* but excitement has a *desire focused on the positive* (what you want to happen) while anxiety has a *desire focused on the negative* (what you do <u>not</u> want to happen).

EMOTIONS AND SITUATIONS

The following sections will show you how *desires* and *expectations* create emotions in familiar everyday situations.

There will be four section headings for these situations.

Work

Relationships

Crises

Games

As you turn to these situations try to see clearly how the situations do <u>not</u> create the emotion. Rather, it is your choice of desire and expectation that does the creating.

WORK

This section is all about work. Work can relate to our jobs and tasks. All these work situations can bring up a variety of **emotions** including **joy, satisfaction, relief, excitement, anxiety, frustration, anger** and **depression.** Here are some typical work related examples.

Pleasurable Results

Work Load

The Assembly Line

Doing a Job

Making an Appointment

Job Loss

PLEASURABLE RESULTS
Relief, Joy and Satisfaction

You want to feel good. Things keep happening in your life. Some turn out good and others bad. But wait! All these feelings of good and bad are emotions that are caused by your goals, desires and expectations. When things turn out good, you have pleasurable results. These can be feelings of relief, joy or satisfaction.

Mr. A, Mr. C and Mrs. B all have taken a test that is very important to them and find out that they have passed.

Before the test Mr. A was very concerned. He really needed to pass this test. He was not sure that he did (anxiety). Then he finds out that he has passed and feels great (relief).

Before the test Mrs. B was pessimistic and believed she probably would not pass the test. When she finds out that she did pass, she is ecstatic (joy).

Before the test Mr. C was very confident that he would pass. After finding out he passed, he feels content and (satisfied).

Looking over this situation, you can realize that expectations made all the difference in the results. All had a strong **desire** to pass. But Mr. A had an uncertain **expectation** and felt relief with the result. Mrs. B had a very low **expectation** and was pleasantly surprised by the result. She felt joy. Finally, Mr. C had a high **expectation** he would pass and felt satisfied with the result.

Before   After

Relief

Joy

Satisfaction

WORKLOAD
Anxiety and Anger

Your workplace can feel overwhelming. When this happens, what goals, desires and expectations do you have?

Look at Mr. A and Miss B. They are facing past work piling up, deadlines and more and more demands. They are both feeling intense pressure. You may feel that you have no choice. You just have to get the work done. This is what Mr. A is feeling.

Mr. A feels a need to get things done. Because of the overwhelming work load, he feels uncertain about being able to do so (anxiety).

Instead of feeling anxious, you may feel resentful of those making demands on you. You simply stop in the middle of your work and comment on the current situation. Miss B does this.

Miss B judges the situation as unfair. She does not like what is happening right now. She strongly needs to be considered and treated fairly. She feels that she is not (anger).

Both Mr. A and Miss B feel a need **(desire)** to get the work done. However, Mr. A. is focused on the work to be done and has an uncertain **expectation** of being able to do it. He feels unsure. He is anxious. Miss B., on the other hand, stops and sees the whole situation as unfair. She has a strong need to be treated fairly but is not getting what she **expects**. <u>She is angry</u>.

THE ASSEMBLY LINE
Anger and Excitement

How about working at a simple job that requires very little attention or thinking on your part? Would you like it? Many people do and many people don't. What makes the difference?

It's your goals, desires and expectations.

Mr. A and Miss B see their assembly line jobs in two different ways.

Mr. A **wants an interesting, challenging job**. He feels a predictable job is boring and a waste of time.

He is very upset that he does not have one. His desire and **expectation is unfulfilled**. He is **angry**.

Miss B, on the other hand, is very happy with the job. She values and **wants a job that is easy and that would allow her to socialize.** Also, a predictable job can bring her a feeling of security.

Miss B **expects** that it is most likely that when she comes to work she will be able to socialize. She is **excited.**

Here we have anger and excitement. It is the same situation but two different emotions. Mr. A has a **desire** for an interesting and challenging job and **expects** that he is stuck and will not get it. He is <u>angry</u>.

Miss B. **wants** a job that will allow her to socialize. With her job, she expects that she is most likely being able to socialize on any given day. The prospects are <u>exciting.</u>

34

DOING A JOB
Anger and Frustration

You have work to do. What are your goals, desires and expectations? If you have difficulty doing your work then emotions can arise. This is the case with Mr. A. He is trying to mow his grass with back pain.

Mr. A is stopped in his tracks by the back pain. He wanted to mow but his back has been hurting. His attention has turned to the pain. He <u>blames</u> the pain and does not want it but he has it (anger).

After stopping and feeling angry about your situation, nevertheless you continue. So like you, Mr. A goes on.

Mr. A is now pushing the mower wanting to get the job done. But the pain is <u>blocking</u> him. This is very upsetting for Mr. A. (frustration.)

Mr. A has a **desire** to get the work done but he is being interrupted. At first he stops and focuses on the past and what has been happening – the pain blocking him. He **expects** to be able to get the work done but has been kept from doing it. He is <u>angry</u>.

He then decides to keep on trying. He is now focused on the future and his desired goal. He **expects** that the pain will lessen and not stop him. But no matter how hard he tries the pain meets him with resistance. He is <u>frustrated</u>.

Anger

Frustration

MAKING AN APPOINTMENT
Anxiety and Frustration

You have an important appointment and do not want to be late. You are in a rush. What are your goals, desires and expectations? Look at Miss A. She is getting off a bus rushing to her appointment.

Miss A. wants to cross the street before the light changes. The light has been green but could change to red any second. She is running and sweating and is not sure that she can make the light before it changes (anxiety).

Suddenly the light changes to red. She cannot cross the street. Now she could be late.

Miss A. stops at the curb in disbelief. She needs to cross but cannot. She is blocked from trying to get to her appointment on time (frustration).

Miss A. **desires** to make her appointment on time. If she doesn't she will need some really good excuses and could be embarrassed. At first her **expectation** is uncertain that she can make the appointment on time. She is anxious.

But then the red light stops her. Now she wants (**desires**) the light to hurry up and change back to green. It is not happening. She is blocked. Her **expectation** of getting to the meeting on time has plunged. She is frustrated.

JOB LOSS
Depression, Anger and Excitement

Do you feel that you could lose your job? How would you feel if
you did? The emotions that you would feel all have to do with
your goals, desires and expectations. Mr. A, Mr. B, Mr. C and Mr.
D have all lost their jobs. Look at how differently each of these
guys sees the situation.

**Mr. A feels devastated. He needed a job and now it is lost
(depression).**

**Mr. B blames himself. He needed the job and feels he did not
perform like he should have (self-directed anger).**

**Mr. C blames the employer. He feels that it was unfair. He
needed the job and it was taken away from him (other-directed
anger).**

You can notice here that anger always has to do with blaming –
either blaming self, others or even just anything.

**Mr. D accepts the verdict. He feels that losing the job is now
an opportunity to find out what he really wants to do
(excitement).**

When you lose a job, you still have a choice on how to frame it.
All these people had a **desire.** However, Mr. A, Mr. B and Mr. C
felt a need to keep their jobs. They all **expected** that there was no
way that they could keep their job. It was over. Mr. A focused on
the loss and felt <u>depressed</u>. Mr. B and Mr. C focused on what they
thought to be the reason for the loss. And they were <u>angry</u>. Mr. D
looked at the loss in quite a different way. He now has a desire to
find out what he really wants to do. He **expects** he can and is
<u>excited</u>.

40

Giving Up
Depression

Self Blame
Anger

Blame Others
Anger

Opportunity
Excitement

KEY POINTS

You may have noticed that your ANXIETY and EXCITEMENT have a lot in common. In both of these emotions, you feel uncertain EXPECTATIONS and are unsure about what will happen. But here is the difference. With anxiety you feel bad because you DESIRE or want to avoid something happening. Your desire is focused on a negative goal. Excitement is quite different. You feel good and are focused on what you want to happen. This DESIRE has a positive goal. (Pages 19-25)

You might find it hard at times to separate your FRUSTRATION and ANGER. One of these emotions can quickly and easily flow into the other. Both have very low EXPECTATIONS that you are getting or have gotten what you DESIRE. When you are frustrated, your focus is on the future and trying to fulfill your goal. But you are being held up or blocked right now. You want to not be blocked. You have a negative goal. On the other hand, you may become angry at something that has just happened or has happened a while ago. Unlike frustration, anger is fueled by the past. You may think something was foolish, unfair or that you were not respected or considered. Nevertheless, when you are angry, you are blaming someone, something or even yourself for what has happened. What you want is for something to not have happened. Like frustration, anger is a negative goal. (Pages 36-37)

42

RELATIONSHIPS

We can feel good or bad about our relationships. This section will point out how we create these feelings in some common situations. The **emotions** include **satisfaction, relief, excitement, anxiety, frustration, anger** and **depression.** Here are some examples of situations that include feelings about yourself and others.

Arguments

Being Alone

Waiting with Jealousy, Impatience and Guilt

Justice

It's What is Inside that Counts

ARGUMENTS
Anger and Frustration

You know we all have different perspectives. So there is bound to be occasional conflict. We are all being just the way we are. Can you accept that? If not, arguments can flare up. The "blame game" begins. Who is right? Who is wrong? Who is at fault? If you are right, it might be even worse. You become even angrier. Finding that you were wrong might make it easier to let go of the anger.

During an argument, the anger can turn into frustration. This can happen when the other person keeps ignoring what you are saying. Anger is all about blame and frustration is all about feeling blocked. In both anger and frustration there is a **desire** to have the other person see things your way. And with that desire is an **expectation** that it is not happening. You can see in the pictures that the age and sex of the participants does not matter. The same emotions arise.

BEING ALONE
Depression and Anxiety

Do you like being alone? You can be alone and not feel lonely.
When you feel lonely you become emotional. Goals, desires and
expectations become involved.

Look at Mr. A and Mr. B? Both Mr. A and Mr. B are alone and
feeling lonely and don't like it. They want or need to have
someone around.

No one likes to feel *lonely, helpless* or *empty.*

Mr. A **needs someone around so that he will not feel empty and
without value**.

He **does not expect** anyone to show up and feels **depressed.**

Mr. B **needs to have someone around so that he will not feel
vulnerable and helpless.**

He is **not sure** that he could get help if he needs it and feels very
anxious.

Do you see what causes the depression and anxiety here? For
depression, Mr. A has a **desire** and really wants company. He
expects that he will not get what he wants. He is depressed.

Unlike Mr. A, Mr. B's **desire** is a need to feel safe while alone.
His **expectation** of being able to be safe is uncertain. He is unsure
and feels anxiety.

WAITING WITH JEALOUSY, IMPATIENCE AND GUILT
Anger, Frustration and Anxiety

Can you remember when you had a hard time waiting? You could have been waiting for a phone call, a ride, an appointment or something else. Whatever it was it could be stressful.

Mrs. A, Miss B, and Miss C are all in the same situation of waiting. They are all waiting for a train. Mrs. A is jealous and compares herself with someone who she feels undeserving.

Mrs. A wants to make an appointment on time and feels it is unfair that an undeserving person will make it on time and she will not (anger).
If you always want and expect things to be fair, you can stay angry for most of your life.

What is happening to Miss. B? She keeps checking her watch and feels impatient. The more you watch time the slower it goes.
Miss B wants to make her meeting on time. The train is late. She feels blocked from getting to her meeting (frustration).

Now Miss C. is feeling something quite different. She would feel responsible and guilty if she misses the meeting. She is really feeling up tight.

Miss C. feels that she needs to make the meeting on time but is not sure she will make it (anxiety).

So you can wait for something in different ways. It all depends on your goals, desires and expectations. Mrs. A, Miss B and Miss C all have a **desire** to make it to an appointment on time. Mrs. A **expects** she will not make it and is <u>angry</u>. Miss B **expects** to be late because she is held up. She is <u>frustrated</u>. Miss C **expects** that she might be late, is uncertain, and feels <u>anxiety</u>.

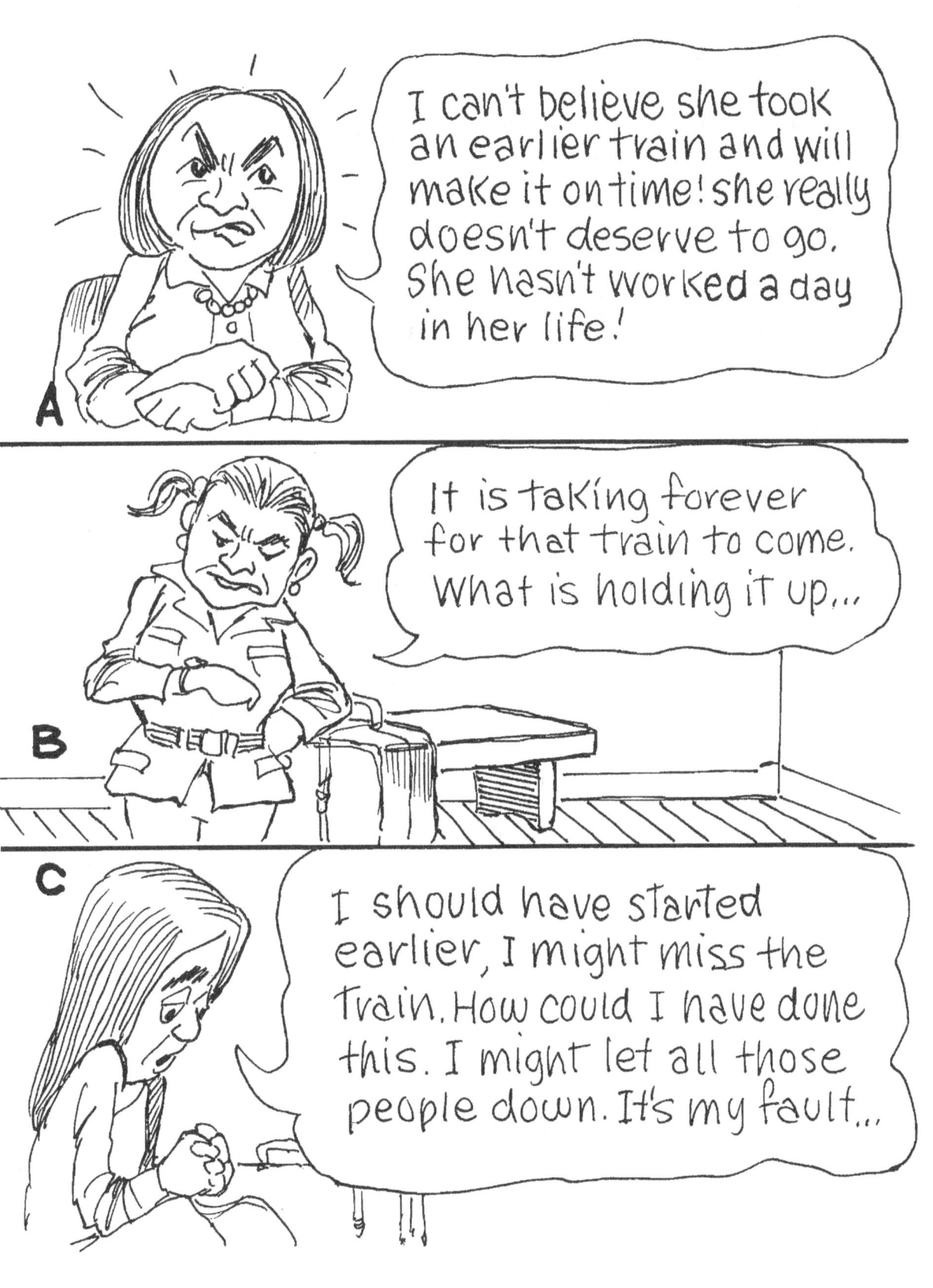

JUSTICE (REVENGE)
Anger and Satisfaction

Can you remember when someone made you really angry and you felt a desire to strike back at that person? And how did you feel when you got your revenge? Notice Mrs. A watching a man with his dog on TV.

Mrs. A sees the man kick the dog and wants justice. She is shocked and blames the man for his insensitivity (anger).

Suddenly, the dog spins around and bites the man. Mrs. A is elated. She feels justice has been served (satisfaction).

Mrs. A has a **desire** for fairness and justice. In fact she **expects** that. When the dog is kicked, she does not get what she **expects**. She is angry. Later when the dog bites the man, she feels her **desire** has been met and she ultimately got what she **wanted** and **expected**. She is satisfied.

This example shows you how easily bad and good feelings can run into one another.

IT'S WHAT IS INSIDE THAT COUNTS
Anxiety, Relief and Excitement

You might think that emotions can be understood by how people act. But we all know that actors can fake emotions and people can cry out of joy or sorrow. Actions do not show us what is at the "heart" of emotions. Instead, we need to go to the inner experience. It's what is inside that counts.

The mother is sending her daughter off to school. The school bus is waiting. The daughter (Little Miss A) does not want to go.

Little Miss A **does not want to get on the bus and have the teacher yell at her.**

She **expects** that the teacher might yell at her and feels **anxious.**

Later, Little Miss A is running off the bus and returning from school. She is so happy to get out of school and is **relieved**.

The mother is fooled by her daughter's happiness and thinks it is because she enjoyed school. She only sees the "outside" of the emotion and not the "inside".

What causes Little Miss A to feel anxious and then relieved and excited? At first she has a **desire** to <u>not</u> be yelled at by her teacher. She is unsure **(uncertain expectation)** as to whether or not this will happen. She is <u>anxious.</u>

Later, Little Miss A has a **desire** to get out of school and play with her friends and **expects** that now it can happen. She is at first <u>relieved</u> and then <u>excited.</u>

KEY POINTS

With DEPRESSION, you have given up and can feel alone and outside of things. Energy and motivation can drop with feelings of despair and hopelessness. Like all the emotions, you can choose to create depression. Just think of something that you really want or need. This could be a positive or negative goal. Hold that desire and even image it. Now, while holding the desire, tell yourself, "there is no way I will ever get it". How do you feel? That is an example of depression. All that you need is a strong DESIRE with an impossible EXPECTATION. Giving up the desire but not the expectation can result in resignation. Acceptance is giving up both your desire and expectation. (Pages 40-41)

DEPRESSION as well as ANGER, FRUSTRATION and ANXIETY can occur with any of the meanings such as being bored, embarrassed, impatient, jealous or guilt-ridden. For example, when you are impatient, you could have the emotion of ANXIETY, FRUSTRATION, ANGER or DEPRESSION. Any common emotion can link up with any one of those meanings. (Pages 24-25, 34-35, 38-39, 48-49)

54

CRISES

In this section we will look at crises. In crises situations we feel threatened. Often they are unpredictable and seem out of our control. But again, the **emotions** we feel such as **relief, excitement, anxiety, anger** and **depression** do not depend on the situations but rather our reactions to these situations. Here are some examples.

Crises and Uncertainty

The Doctor's Office

Claustrophobia and Fear of Heights

Motivation for Change

CRISES AND UNCERTAINTY
Anxiety, Fear and Shock

Uncertainty can be very disturbing. It is a big part of anxiety, fear and shock. Often you would like life to be predictable. It would give you a sense of stability and security. But life is uncertain. The future is "not yet." This uncertainty is most obvious during crises.

Mr. A is riding his motorcycle on a curvy country road. Suddenly, a truck appears to be about to enter the road.

Mr. A sees this up ahead and does <u>not</u> want to have an accident. He is not sure if the truck will enter the road or not (anxiety).

The truck cuts right in front of him as he tries not to hit it.

Mr. A does <u>not</u> want to hit the truck and swerves to the left. In this immediate situation, he doesn't know if he will avoid the crash (fear).

He has avoided the crash but is now headed over a cliff.

Mr. A is stunned and completely out of control. All that is left is uncertainty of whether he will be injured or killed (shock).

In a crisis, you can feel anxiety, fear or shock. At first, Mr. A did <u>not</u> want (**desire**) to have an accident but he did not know what to **expect**. He was <u>anxious</u>. Next he wanted (**desire**) to avoid the immediate contact with the truck but was not sure he could. His **expectation** was uncertain and he had <u>fear</u>. Finally, he was headed over the cliff and simply filled with the **expectation** of uncertainty. He was in <u>shock</u>.

CRISES AND UNCERTAINTY (continued)

Suppose you are at the theater and a fire breaks out. Now it does matter where you are seated. Are you close to the exits, in the middle or back of the theater or worse yet seated in the balcony? The fire rages and the uncertainty of escape is stifling.

Before the fire, the movie is boring for Mr. and Mrs. A. They wonder "when will it ever end", "what a waste of time" and "why am I here?" Anger, frustration and depression set in.

Then the fire erupts!

People run for the exits in panic. Those that feel the hot flames whipping at their backs run for their lives. And then there are those in the balcony. They are filled with uncertainty and no possibility of escape.

Mr. and Mrs. A flee for the exits. They feel the urgent need to escape now. They are not sure they can (fear).

Meanwhile Mr. and Mrs. B are stuck in the balcony with no means of escape. They can only hope that the fire will not reach them.

Mr. and Mrs. B feel stuck without any way to escape. They simply must wait with uncertainty and see what happens (shock).

In this crisis, there is a strong **desire** to survive. You are faced with either the uncertain **expectation** of escape or the uncertain **expectation** of the outcome. Mr. and Mrs. A are not sure of escape while Mr. and Mrs. B are not sure of the outcome. All and all, when it comes to crises, it is all about uncertainty, the hallmark of fear and <u>anxiety</u>.

THE DOCTOR'S OFFICE
Depression, Anger, Anxiety, Fear and Relief

You go to the doctor's office to get your test results. You are concerned and a whole bunch of emotions run through you. This is Mr. A's situation.

Mr. A does not want a bad test result. At first he considers the entire catastrophe. It is the worst thing that could happen. He has a terrible disease. There is no chance that he will get the result that he wants (depression).

A moment later Mr. A wonders why this is happening to him. It seems so unfair. He blames life for its unfairness (anger).

Next Mr. A realizes that he does not really know what the test results will show. He is not sure he will get the result he so desperately wants. He wonders about his options (anxiety).

Then the doctor enters the room with his test results.
Now Mr. A has what he fears right in front of him. The immediate uncertainty is overwhelming (fear).

The doctor hands you the results and they show that you are fine.
Mr. A is relieved and feels great (relief).

You can see how the emotions change with desires and expectations. Throughout the wait Mr. A has a **desire** to not have a bad result. At first his **expectation** of getting his desire fulfilled is zero (depression). As he sits in the doctors office his emotions change. Next he blames life for his predicament and feels anger. After this, he feels an uncertain **expectation** with the whole situation (anxiety and fear). Finally, he gets a good result and has a certain **expectation** that he will be OK. He feels relief.

1.

2.

3.

4.

5.

6.

CLAUSTROPHOBIA AND FEAR OF HEIGHTS
Anxiety and Relief

How do you feel about enclosed and high places? Does it bother you to climb a ladder, walk on a roof or fly in a plane? What about going deeply into a cave or being trapped in a large crowd of people? With claustrophobia you don't like feeling trapped or suffocated. The fear of heights is the opposite. You don't like the feeling of an open space and the lack of feeling secure, stable and grounded.

A mother is taking her son and daughter on a glass elevator which goes up and down the outside of a large hotel building. The daughter has a fear of heights and the son has claustrophobia. In the elevator, the mother asks both of them to look through the glass at the city below.

Little Miss A does <u>not</u> want to look at the city below. She feels shaky and that she might fall (anxiety).
Little Mr. B likes to look through the glass and see all the open space. He does <u>not</u> want to feel trapped and now he feels breathing room (relief).

Next, the mother asks both her kids to focus on the glass walls of the elevator.
Suddenly, Little Miss A feels secure. She does not want to feel unstable and now she feels safe (relief).
Little Mr. B, on the other hand, feels trapped by the glass walls. He does not want to feel that he cannot escape. But he is unsure and uncertain that he will be able to escape (anxiety).

Both Little Miss A and Little Mr. B do <u>not</u> want (**desire**) to experience what they fear. Both feel uncertain (**expectation**) when faced with their fears. They feel <u>anxiety</u>.
When they both change their focus, their **desire** to avoid the fearful experience remains but now they feel confident and **expect** that they have avoided what scares them <u>(relief)</u>.

62

MOTIVATION FOR CHANGE
Anger, Excitement and Depression

What is your attitude toward all the crises in the world? There is overpopulation, global warming, health care issues, terrorism and possible economic collapse. Are you someone who has lost faith in people and given up? Do you see hope and respond by trying to problem solve? Or do you put your "head in the sand" and just focus on your own day to day life?

Mr. A is disgusted. Disgust is a form of anger with the volume (desire) turned down. He wanted leaders to take care of things but they didn't. He feels that we, humanity, have really messed things up and now there is no hope. So, just live it up! Buy on credit. Use up all the resources until they run out. It does not matter. He has given up (anger).

Mr. B wants to do what he can to change himself as well as others. He has hope. He knows he can try. He enjoys the challenge and feels confident that he can work things out and solve problems (excitement).

Mr. C just feels helpless and wants to block things out. He may complain from time to time but he is too busy living his own life to pay attention. He would rather watch movies instead of the news. He feels he can't do anything anyway and simply feels resignation (depression).

Mr. A and Mr. C both <u>desire</u> change but feel their <u>expectations</u> will not be fulfilled. Therefore they have lessened their desires for change and Mr. A has moved from <u>anger</u> to disgust and Mr. C has moved from <u>depression</u> to resignation. Mr. B is quite different. He sees the crises but has hope. This is because he understands that the future is never closed. He wants (<u>desire</u>) to try and solve problems and <u>expects</u> that he can. He is <u>excited</u>.

KEY POINTS

When you are in crises or risky situations, the most common bad emotion is ANXIETY and its relatives fear and shock. These three feelings all have uncertain EXPECTATIONS to match the uncertainty of the situations. When you feel anxiety and fear, you have a negative goal-you DESIRE or want to avoid something. But have you noticed that when what you are anxious about becomes very immediate-like it is happening right now-it becomes fear. And then what about if you feel that you have lost all control? There is nothing that you can do about the situation. You cannot avoid it. You have no choice but to wait and see what happens. The uncertainty is still there but without the goal. Then you can be in shock! (Pages 56-63)

How can you remove and abolish these bad emotions. One suggestion would be to become aware of the *present* while accepting and embracing the reality of whatever is happening. Remember, uncertainty lives in the future and not the present. Another suggestion would be to take action to remove uncertainty. Remember the example (on pages 20-21) where although the passenger is very uncertain and anxious, the driver is confident and busy operating the car. When you are busy doing what you know you can do, there is less mental space for anxiety and its relatives fear and shock to appear.

GAMES

We all play games. Games have to do with winning and losing.
This section will show you how emotions can relate to game
situations. A whole range of **emotions** including **satisfaction,
excitement, anxiety, anger and depression** can come up in these
situations. Here are some examples.

The Stock Market

Risk Taking and Winning

Confidence and Overconfidence

Setting Yourself Up

THE STOCK MARKET
Excitement and Anger

Would you agree that greed is one of our biggest problems in society? We often become very angry at greedy people. But just as often we may not see it in ourselves. We may feel justified and even excited about the prospect of getting more and more. Playing the stock market is focused on one thing – making money.

Mr. A loves money. It can buy him lots of things, even people. You can love the power money gives you.

Mr. A wants to make money so he can have all kinds of things that would make him happy. He expects that he will be able to do this since his stock just soared (excitement).

On the other hand, you might look at Mr. A as greedy. He is not helping anyone else, only himself. This is how Mr. B sees it.

Mr. B does <u>not</u> want Mr. A to make money in the stock market. He blames him for being selfish, greedy and wrapped up only in himself. However, he sees that Mr. A's stock just soared. Mr. B did not get what he wanted (anger).

Mr. A has a **desire** to have many things and **expects** that he will be able to have them. He is <u>excited</u>. Mr. B has a **desire** for Mr. A to fail at making more money. However, Mr. A does make more money and Mr. B's desire and **expectation** is unfulfilled. Mr. B is resentful and <u>angry</u>.

RISK TAKING AND WINNING
Excitement, Anxiety and Depression

What happens when you take a risk? What goals, desires and expectations may be involved and how will you feel about it? What is it you focus on – the process or the result?

If the odds of winning are low you may or may not play. If you enjoy the playing you are likely to take the risk. You are <u>not</u> focused on your chances of winning. Your goal is simply to play to have a chance of winning! Focus is on the process and not the result.

This is what Mr. A is doing. He wants to win but is focused on just playing and having fun (excitement).

What happens if you really need the money and need to win? This can be real scary. You believe you have a chance but you are not sure. If you are real desperate then you will probably take the chance.

This is Mr. B. He gives it a shot but feels very shaky (anxious).

You may need to win but feel that you have little or no chance. So you feel "Oh well. I got to try." You take the chance.

Mr. C feels the need to win but senses a kind of hopelessness (depression).

Do you see what causes the emotions here? Mr A has a **desire** and wants to play with a chance to win and **expects** that he can do this. He is <u>excited</u>. Mr. B has a **desire** and needs to win but feels an uncertain **expectation** of being able to do so. He is <u>anxious</u>. Finally, Mr. C has a **desire** and needs to win but **expects** that it will not happen. He is <u>depressed</u>.

CONFIDENCE AND OVERCONFIDENCE
Satisfaction and Complacency

Do you believe that you can do something or that you will do it? If so, you feel confident. But what happens when you take things for granted? When this happens you can slip into overconfidence.

Look at Mr. A the baseball player. He is confident. He wants to win and believes if he makes the effort that he will win. He is (satisfied) with what he can do and will do.

Here you understand that you have the ability to win and have an opportunity to win. You feel good about yourself and the situation.

Now look at Mr. B. a baseball manager. He appears very confident. He wants to win and feels like winning is a "done deal". Because he is so sure of himself and self satisfied, his desire to win is weakened. He becomes (complacent).

In this situation, you believe that little or no effort will be required to win. You become overconfident.

Satisfaction and complacency can be closely related. Mr. A has a **desire** to win and feels <u>satisfied</u> with his preparation. His **expectation** of winning is certain. Mr. B also **expects** to win but feels little or no effort is necessary to do so. All he has to do is show up. Because of his overconfidence, his **desire** to make the *effort* to win drops. This drop in the intensity of desire can move satisfaction to a lower level, that of <u>complacency</u>.

SETTING YOURSELF UP
Excitement, Anxiety, Depression and Anger

There is an old saying, "When you greatly desire something then the more you expect to get it the greater the disappointment if you don't get it."

It is important to understand how you set yourself up to feel good or bad. You do this with your desires and expectations.

Mr. A, Mr. B and Mr. C are watching a football game. It is the last play of the game and their team has a chance to win. Mr. A and Mr. B really want to win. Mr. C is laid back with very little desire.

Mr. A is confident and expects his team to score (excitement).

Mr. B can hardly watch. He feels uncertain about what will happen and is focused on the possible negative outcome (anxiety).

Mr. C is just interested in seeing what will happen. He is uncertain about what will happen with almost no desire (interested and relaxed).

Their team is stopped and they lose the game!

Mr. A is intensely depressed. What a let down! He is very disappointed.

Mr. B is angry at the team for letting him down. But he kind of expected it and does not feel as disappointed as Mr. A.

Mr. C considers it only a game and goes on. The result had very little importance to him.

There you have it. Mr. A had a strong **desire** and high **expectation** and was greatly disappointed and depressed. Mr. B **had** a strong **desire** and an uncertain **expectation** and was angry rather than devastated. Mr. C was unaffected.

So what about being optimistic? This seems like it could be a set up. However, it is not a problem as long as you desire what you have control over. Then your result is more likely to happen. You could even be excited.

2

KEY POINTS

Bad emotions and good emotions can also turn into one another. Some examples are ANGER can turn into SATISFACTION and ANXIETY can suddenly result in RELIEF. This shows you how good and bad emotions can be closely connected. All depends on your DESIRE and EXPECTATION related to what you are focused on. (Pages 50-51, 62-63)

Your EXPECTATIONS before something happens can actually affect your emotions after it happens. An interesting rule is that *given you desire something very much, the more you expect to get it the greater your disappointment (frustration, anger or depression) if you do not get it. The reverse is also true. The less you expect to get it the greater your happiness (joy, satisfaction or relief) if you do get it.* (Pages 30-31, 74-77)

You can't find the *causes* of emotions outside yourself in behavior or the environment. These causes occur inside yourself and you can understand and identify them by being aware of and noticing your own thoughts, feelings and beliefs. (Pages 52-53)

Most often, awareness (observation) and deep understanding will be enough for desired change to take place.

78

WRAP UP

We have shown you many common situations when emotions arise. And what you have learned is that, although situations can *powerfully influence* emotions, they do <u>not</u> *cause* them. The causes of emotions are <u>in you</u>. Now, don't ever blame yourself. It is not your fault, it is <u>not you</u>. It is the mind/brain machine that is <u>in you</u>. It is running on automatic programs from the past. With the help of your observer and the information in this little book, you can learn how to take control of your emotions.

Here are the mechanics of the mind/brain machine.

When **desires** are high and things are important to you, then emotions are easily created. When desires are low then your emotional life is turned down. Desire turns the volume and intensity up or down on your emotions.

Expectations can determine what kind of emotion you will have. We have presented eight common high volume/intense emotions with their expectations.

<u>Good Emotions</u>
Joy - What you want to happen is happening.
Expectation is certain that you are getting what you want.

Satisfaction - What you <u>want</u> to happen did happen or will happen.
Expectation is certain that you got or will get what you want.

Relief - What you <u>need</u> to happen did happen or will happen.
Expectation is certain that you got or will get what you need.

Excitement - What you want to happen may or may not happen.
Expectation is uncertain.

Bad Emotions

Anxiety – What you need to have happen may or may not happen.
Expectation is uncertain.

Frustration – What you want or need to have happen now
(remove the *block*) is <u>not</u> happening.
Expectation of getting the block removed <u>now</u> is zero.

Anger – What you want is to <u>not</u> have had something happen.
You place *blame* on someone, something or yourself for not
getting what you wanted or needed.
Expectation of getting what you wanted or needed is zero.

Depression – What you want or need did <u>not</u> happen or will <u>not</u>
happen.
Expectation of getting what you want or need is zero.

We all know how these emotions can affect the body and health.
Good emotions can result in good physical health. Bad emotions
can result in poor physical health. Here are some interesting
connections.

Is your stomach feeling shaky, uneasy and uncertain? Maybe it is
related to the *uncertainty* in *anxiety*. What about the blockage in
heart disorders and the *block* in *frustration*? There is also the
painful tightness in low back pain and the *tight* holding pattern in
anger. And cancer reflected in the giving up of the immune and
defense systems of the body could easily relate to the *giving up* in
depression.

Once you start to understand your emotions and how they can
affect your health and well-being, what can you do to change
things?

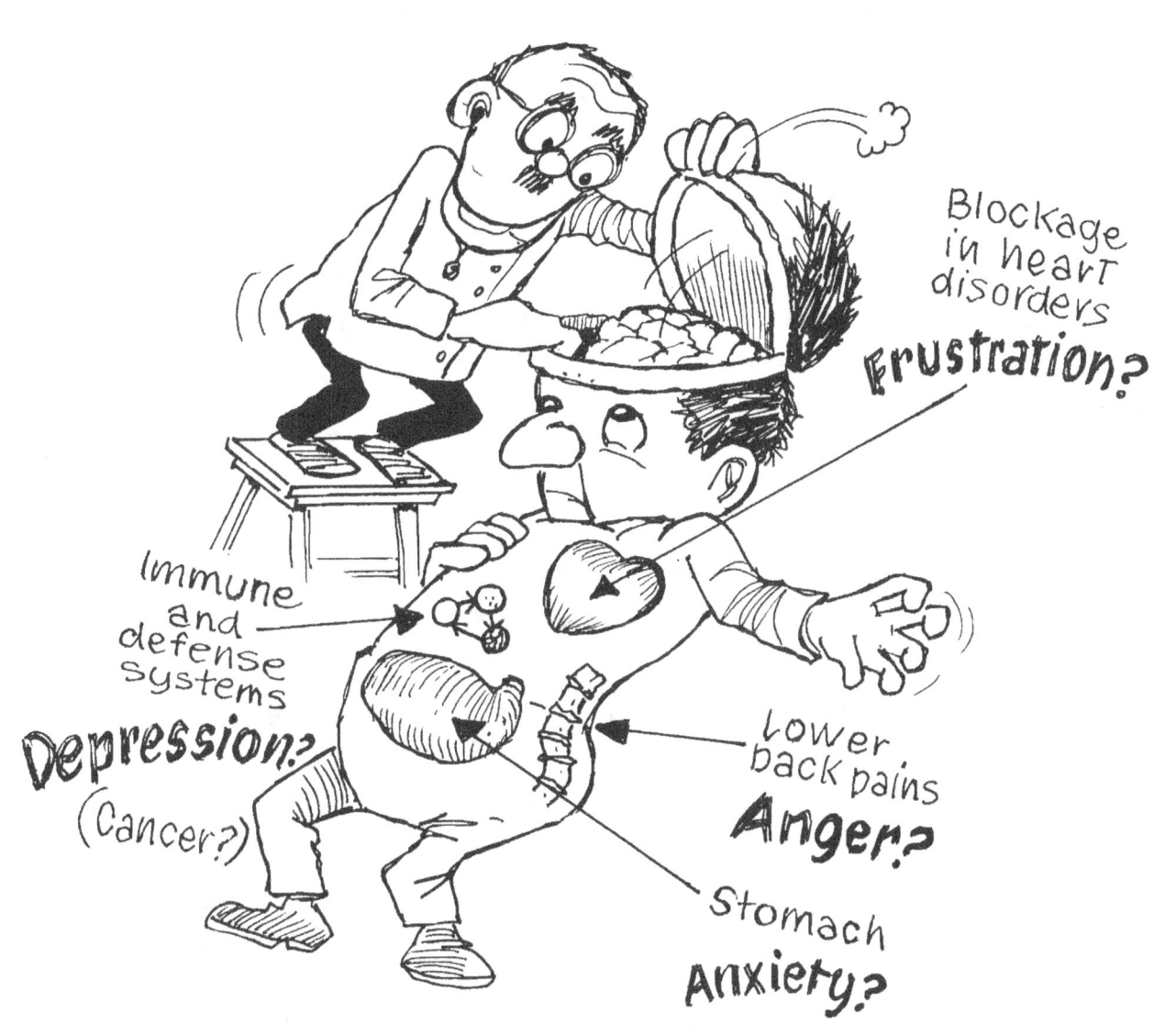

You can begin by learning how to notice and be the observer of your inner life. When you "look inside", ask yourself - What do I want, how much do I want it and what is my expectation of getting it? This means you have to notice your thoughts, values and even some of your deeper underlying beliefs. This is not easy. Take your time. Don't rush it. The benefits of an accurate assessment are great! When you have answered those questions, that's it! Then you will have found what is behind your emotions. You have learned how emotions are caused by two main factors in the mind/brain machine - **Desire and Expectation**. This understanding is the first step to change.

The next step includes two ways that you can impact your desires and expectations and increase the chances of good emotions.

1. **Choose a <u>DESIRED</u> positive goal.** This is something you really want and not something that you want to avoid.

2. **Choose a goal that has a high <u>EXPECTATION</u> of success**. This is something that you know you can do. Remember outcomes are not under your control!

Only through changing desires and expectations will emotions change.

You now have all the tools necessary to understand and take control of your emotions or your "horse". Once the driver gets the information (desires, goals and expectations) from the observer and understands the horse, the driver can get the cart on the road to a better life. ***Good emotions or bad emotions, it is your choice.***

Jim Barrell
Teacher, Researcher, Consultant, Speaker

Jim obtained his PhD in experimental psychology at the University of California at Davis. He has taught at University of Florida and was a tenured full professor at University of West Georgia. His other affiliations include the Medical College of Virginia, National Institutes of Health and Stanford Research Institute International. He has researched human emotions for over 30 years and has published numerous articles and books as well as given many presentations at conferences related to the unique discovery of actual laws of human emotions. Currently, Jim is consulting for business and sports organizations as well as conducting workshops.

Art Maynor
Publisher, Artist, Teacher, Historian

Art was born in Ybor City, Florida. He has lived all his life within twenty minutes of where he was born and raised. He graduated from the University of Tampa with a BS in education. Art has worked graphically in all media; print, television, outdoor, audio-visual etc. He has also worked in the fields of education, business, and publications and currently enjoys his new venture into the internet. Art's past works have included film strips, video tapes and the publication of numerous illustrated mini books.